*It's never t[oo] save for retirement !
But, earlier is much better !! !*

Retirement Investments 101:

Mutual Funds
4/2/2015

King A. Kovacs

First Edition: Printed September 2012
Second Edition: Printed July 2013
Third Edition: Printed January 2014
Fourth Edition: Printed January 2015
Copyright 1999-2015 by King A. Kovacs
Mutual Interest Data Service, Ltd. www.largedividends.com
All rights reserved
EAN-13: 9780615669823

CreateSpace, North Charleston, South Carolina

Introduction

This revised and expanded guide book is written for individual investors striving for prosperity and continuance of wealth for retirement years. The primary goal, help build and increase savings and/or retirement "nest eggs".

Retirement Investments 101: Mutual Funds provides unbiased and verifiable data on where there is "money" to be found and how to "find value" among thousands of mutual funds being offered. This is a financial working tool that can be used to help increase your personal financial prosperity.

Every year, the best 350 mutual funds from a data base, which was established and maintained since 1999, are presented to the reader.

There are 32 exclusive and detailed reports of the mutual fund performances, gains & losses, distributions, and returns. These reports represent 32 mutual fund investment categories.

This is a working tool to be used and benefited from when making retirement investments.

CONTENTS

MUTUAL FUND REPORTS.................... 21

BOND FUND REPORTS........................... 71

RETIREMENT PROSPERITY.................... 89

About the Author.................................. 95

RETIREMENT:

Being middle aged, or older, in good health and a Wage earner; take advantage investing in one of the best return investments, an Individual Retirement Account (IRA) which is a savings account. Time waits for no one. All of us are getting a little older every year. It is essential to plan for the future and prepare for your retirement now, not tomorrow. This can be achieved by establishing a goal, making a commitment and being perseverant.

Establishing Goal:

There are many types of investments to consider in your retirement plans. However; the investment in this book will be limited to mutual funds. A good starting point is to determine the type of mutual fund investments that should be in your portfolio and the risks involved. Should the assets be aggressive, con-servative or moderate? Will the investments be low risk, below average risk, average risk, above average risk or high risk?

Aggressive: is a method of portfolio management and asset allocation that seeks to achieve maximum return. An aggressive investment strategy attempts to grow assets at above-average rate compared to its industry or the overall market. The risk can range from average to high.

Conservative an investment strategy that aims to grow invested capital over the long-term. This strategy focuses on minimizing risk by making long-term invest-ments in companies that show consistent growth over time. Conservative growth mutual funds have low asset turnover or a high percentage of fixed assets on the balance sheets and use a buy-hold investment strategy. The risk varies from low to average.

Moderate investments try to reduce risks and increase returns equally. The investment may incur a short-term loss of principal and lower degree of liquidity in exchange for long-term appreciation. Typical risk in this kind of investment are average to above-average

2

Commitment:

To succeed in the endeavor, the investor has to decide how much money will be saved and invested. He or she has to determine whether it will be weekly, bi-weekly or monthly? Investors must be as diligent as possible in keeping to their promise. After the initial IRA shares a r e purchased, there are varying minimums of IRA additional purchases that can be made. For example, some funds have a minimum of $50. Other mutual funds have a minimum of $1000 or more.

Perseverance:

We all know how difficult it is to save money; especially when encountering hard times. However; the investor has to be persistent in saving as much money as they can, even under those conditions.

When experiencing this kind of situation, modifying the commitment of how often to purchase additional mutual fund shares should be made. Once the crisis ceases to exist, resume the normal retirement savings of purchasing more fund shares.

INDIVIDUAL RETIREMENT ACCOUNT

What is an Individual Retirement Account? The title is self-explanatory, but it is one of the best investment vehicles offered to individuals planning to retire. As owner of the accounts you are the portfolio manager of your individual retirement account and its success or failure.

You manage, direct, control and create the assets in the investment. You decide whether the investment will be aggressive, moderate, or conservative. You deter-mine how much money will be invested each week or month.

The following guidelines must be adhered to as required by the Internal Revenue Service.

*IRA Contribution Limits:
For 2015 the maximum you can contribute to all of your traditional and Roth IRA is $5500, if you are under 50. The maximum is $6500, if you are 50 or older. . .

*IRS Withholding Calculator:
This easy-to-use calculator can help you figure your federal income tax withholding so your employer can withhold the correct amount from your pay. This is particularly helpful if you had too much withheld in the past, your situation has changed, or you are starting a new job. . .

*Tax information for individuals:
For 2015 the maximum you can contribute to all of your traditional and Roth IRA is the smaller of $5500, if you are under 50 years of age.   The   maximum   is $6500, if you are 50 or older. . .

*IRA Contribution after age 70½:
You cannot make regular contributions to a traditional

IRA if you're age 70½ or older. However; you can still contribute to a Roth IRA and make rollover contributions to a Roth or traditional IRA regardless of your age. . .

*Claiming tax deduction for IRA contribution:
Your traditional IRA contributions may be tax deductible. The deduction may be limited if you or your spouse are covered by a retirement plan at work and your income exceeds certain levels. . .

*Roth IRA contribution limit:
The same general contribution limit applies to both Roth and traditional IRAs. However, your Roth IRA contribution might be limited based on your filing status and income. . .

*Spousal IRAs:
If you file a joint return, you and your spouse can each make IRA contributions even if only one of you has taxable compensation. The amount of your combined contributions cannot be more than the taxable compensation reported on your joint return. It does not matter which spouse earned the compensation.

*Source: Internal Revenue Service   http://www.irs.gov/Retirement-Plans/Plan-Participant,-Employee/Retirement-Topics-IRA-Contribution-Limits

Best news of all. Reinvested income and capital gains distributed by an IRA mutual fund are not subject to being taxed as long as you do not withdraw a cent from the account.

IRA income will not be considered as income tax until reaching the age of 70½. At that time, you must withdraw a minimum amount of distribution from your IRA portfolio once reaching the age of 70½. This is a normal distribution and is taxable for the year of withdrawal because it is income.

Required Minimum Distribution The mutual funds that are in your IRA portfolio will inform you of the distribution that you must with draw from your account based on the RMD calculator_results.

Important Decisions: Your IRA portfolio planning, controlling and managing is entirely in your hands. You make the decision of the portfolio's IRA asset allocations which are investments based on your goals and risk tolerance.

Example: An IRA portfolio might consist of 10% growth stocks, 40% equity mutual funds, 50% bond funds. The investments in a IRA portfolio are completely in your hands.

Effective 2015, when a mutual fund is not performing up to your satisfaction, you can rollover a maximum of one mutual fund per year into another more successful mutual fund.

MUTUAL FUNDS

What is a mutual fund?

A mutual fund in the United States is an investment that is regulated by the Securities & Exchange Commission and listed on the NASDAQ market. Being an investment company, mutual funds are in business of collecting funds from investors and pooling the assets for the purpose of building a portfolio of securities according to stated objectives in the prospectus.

What is a open-end mutual fund?
Funds that issue shares continuously and they must repurchase them from shareholders on demand. The majority of mutual funds available to investors are open-end.

What is a closed-end mutual fund?
Funds issuing shares in large blocks and limited intervals. The mutual funds are not obligated to redeem or repurchase them.

There are four basic types of mutual funds: 1) money market, 2) stock or equity, 3) bond and 4) hybrid. Money market: these are mutual funds that invest in short-term securities. This would include treasury bills, commercial paper and certificates of deposit. Stock/equity, bond, and hybrid funds invest in long-term securities. Hybrid funds invest in a combination of stocks, bonds and other securities.

It is important to note that mutual funds <u>are not</u> guaranteed by the government or FDIC. There are no guarantees of future performance. Always contact the mutual fund and read the fund's prospectus Investment Facts: This type of information is essential when searching for successful investments.

To best protect your nest egg, it is prudent to make decisions based on proven long-term positive years of gains versus the number of years of losses. Performance gains should be the nucleus of your retirement investment.

Of course, there are many other factors that come into play before making an investment. Consideration has to be given to mutual fund fees, minimum purchase, percentage of gain, percentage of loss, etc.

Tools of the trade enable individuals in any profession to excel in the pursuit of their endeavor. One of the best tools available in the financial field is being familiar with the mutual fund's ticker symbol and putting it to use. The ticker symbol_is your key to a wealth of investment facts.   An example would be Van Eck Emerging Markets, the ticker symbol is GBFAX.

Investment Facts:

Most Internet financial search engines provide information that is needed to make decisions based on facts. To view the vast resource of mutual fund data, which is readily available if the ticker symbol is known. Search engines like Yahoo or Google simply require the ticker symbol being placed into the QUOTE dialog box. Here is a thumbnail sketch of the invaluable data and facts that are provided.

Profile: Lists the mutual fund's family, address, toll free phone number, portfolio manager name and tenure, mutual fund's inception, fund's net assets, investment fund category and investment objectives.

Purchase: Includes the mutual fund's minimum initial purchase, minimum initial IRA purchase, minimum subsequent purchases, maximum 12b1 fee,and maximum front and sales load (if any).

Performance: Provides the percentage of performance of gain or loss when the fund net asset value is more or less than the opening share price. The net asset value is the current market value of the mutual fund assets per share. The market value of a fund is also referred to as share price. A mutual fund share price is reduced by the amount of distribution and/or lower performance. A net asset value computation is performed daily at the end of each trading day based on the closing market prices of the portfolio's securities.

Total Return: Includes the dividend distribution of income and/or capital gains and the performance of the mutual fund. The dividends and interest earned by a mutual fund on its investment is the income. The dividend distribution of income is usually declared quarterly i.e. March, June, September and December. Many mutual funds declare distribution of capital gains during the month of December. On the day of trade, the share price is decreased by the same amount of distribution (dividends or capital gains) given to shareholders. If, for example a two dollar distribution was declared, the net asset value of the mutual fund would be reduced by two dollars at the close of the market.

11

Top Holdings: Section reveals the top 10 holdings by name of investment and the percent of assets purchased. The asset allocation which includes portfolio percentage of stocks, cash and bonds is also provided. In addition, you see the type of assets included such as technology, financial, healthcare, etc.

Risk: This shows the risk level of a mutual fund attempt to achieve its investment objective. Is the fund a low risk, below risk, average risk, above average risk, or a high risk? The 3-year and 5-year alpha rating and beta rating are also included.

Return Chart: Displays the value of a $10,000 investment of a mutual fund's ticker symbol selected. The chart shows what the current value of a $10,000 purchase of the specific mutual fund would be for one year, three years, five years and even ten years. In addition to this factual data, the chart also shows the ups and downs in value during the time period selected.

Mutual Fund Category:
Listed below are the various types of investment objective categories that mutual funds serve.

Convertible Securities - funds investing in convertible bonds or preferred stocks that pay regular interest and can be converted into shares of common stock.

Balance – Funds investing in stocks, equities and bonds. Primary goal is to maintain a balanced portfolio.

12

Emerging Markets – Funds investing in emerging market equity securities.

Equity Income – Funds seeking high current income and growth by investing in equities.

European Region - Funds investing in markets that are in the European region.

Flexible Income - Funds investing in bonds, convertible securities, limited stocks.

Global Stock - Funds investing in securities traded outside of the United States.

Gold - Funds investing in gold mines, gold coins, bullion.

Health/Bio Technology - Funds investing in Companies related to healthcare, medicine and bio technology.

International Stock - Funds investing in Canadian; international markets.

Large-Cap Core - Funds investing in large companies with independence in the type of shares purchased.

Large-Cap Growth – Funds investing large companies with long-term earnings that are anticipated to grow faster than the earnings of stocks in major indices.

Large–Cap Value - Funds investing in large companies that are recognized as being undervalued compared to major stock indices.

Mid-Cap Core - Funds investing in mid-size companies, with freedom in the type of shares purchased.

Mid-Cap Growth-Funds investing n mid-size companies with long-term earnings that are anticipated to grow faster than the earnings of stocks in major indices.

Mid–Cap Value - funds investing in mid-size companies that are recognized as being undervalued compared to major stock indices.

Mixed–Assets Targeted Allocation – Conservative - Funds investing mainly in U.S. government and corporate income securities and dividend paying common stocks.

Mixed–Assets Targeted Allocation - Growth - Funds investing in stocks, fixed-income securities and cash. Goal is to maintain balance between stocks and fixed income securities.

Mixed–Assets Targeted Allocation -Moderate - Funds investing in stocks, bonds, and corporate income securities.

Multi-Cap Core - Fundsinvesting in various sized companies with independence in the type of shares bought.

Multi-Cap Growth - Funds investing in companies of various sizes, with long-term earnings that are anticipated to grow faster than the earnings of stocks in major indices.

Multi-Cap Value - Funds investing in various sized companies that are recognized as being undervalued compared to major stock indices.

Sector - Funds investing in specific classifications such as banking, food and agriculture, leisure, science and technology, health, utility, etc.

Small-Cap Core - Funds investing in small com panies, with flexibility in the type of shares purchased.

Small-Cap Growth - Funds investing in small companies, with long-term earnings that are anticipated to grow faster than the earnings of stocks in major indices.

Small-Cap Value - Funds investing in small companies that are recognized as being under-valued compared to major stock indices.

Utilities: Funds investing in utility stocks.

Bond Fund Category:

Corporate Grade A Debt - Funds investing in corporate bonds with A credit rating.

Corporate Grade BBB Debt - Funds investing in corporate bonds with BBB credit rating.

General Municipal - Funds investing in states on a national municipal debt level.

General U.S. Taxable - funds investing in general bonds.

High-Yield Taxable - Funds investing in fixed income securities that have high current yields.

High-Yield Municipal - Funds investing in bonds that yield high returns.

Intermediate Bond - Funds investing in investment grade debt issues with maturities 5 to 10 years.

Intermediate Municipal - Funds investing in intermediate-term municipal debt including single states.

Intermediate U.S. - Funds investing in intermediate U.S. Government; U.S. Treasury.

Mortgage - Funds investing in adjustable rate Mortgage; U.S. Mortgage; GNMA.

Multi-Sector Bond - Funds seeking income by asset diversification among fixed–income sectors, usually corporate bonds, foreign bonds and high yield debt securities.

All investment facts can be easily verified once you read the mutual fund's prospectus, which is must reading. The above data is a thumb nail sketch of the invaluable resource that is unlocked with the key of a mutual fund ticker symbol. Isn't this the type of vital information you need to build the secure and prosperous financial retirement for your future?

Distribution:
Shareholders that receive mutual fund distributions have the option to reinvest the income and avoid paying tax, if it's an IRA account. Or, they can opt to receive full payment of the distribution. This would be create a taxable event even if the fund is an IRA account.

When a fund sells an investment security for a higher price than originally paid, the fund has a capital gain. A capital loss is realized when the fund sells an investment security for a lower price than originally paid. If the investment security is held by the fund for more than one year, the gain or loss will be a long-term capital gain or loss.

When the investment security is held by the fund for less than one year, the gain or loss will be a short-term capital gains and loss.

Mutual fund gains and losses are netted together and when the fund has a net gain, that gain is usually distributed to the shareholder once a year. By law, mutual funds must pay out income and realized capital gains to shareholders. These types of distribution are taken from the fund's assets which results in the net asset value being reduced by the same amount as the distribution pay out.

Dollar-cost-averaging: Occurs when you invest at regular intervals despite the market conditions being up or down. This type of investment can help in the long-term because you are purchasing shares at various prices reflecting the ups and downs of the market.

Mutual funds are long-term investments for building assets especially in IRAs and should be timed in years not months or weeks. A mutual fund's portfolio is structured and maintained to achieve the investment objectives that are within its prospectus. Before investing in a mutual fund, you want to know the performance, the return on the long-term, income and capital gains distribution, and the risk.

Having this knowledge can result in maximizes gains in a positive market and minimize losses in a negative market. Being a prudent investor you also want to consider successful mutual funds and you have to be a committed investor for the long-term.

Outstanding Mutual Fund Principle

Mutual funds that are successful year after year have these characteristics:

1. Above average performance
2. Large distribution of income and capital gains
3. Average or low-risk.

Mutual funds that meet these standards can provide investors a nest egg to build and to grow over the long–term to help achieve your retirement objectives.

MUTUAL FUND REPORTS

In the early 90s, I undertook an extensive research project searching for mutual funds that fulfilled three criteria. Every mutual fund investment performance had to consist of: 1) Average or Low Risk, 2) High Returns and 3) Large Dividend Distribution.

Burning the midnight oil and analyzing thousands of mutual funds; a data bank was established of 350 mutual funds meeting on this requirement. The purpose was to build a retirement investment portfolio foundation that would grow and prosper for myself and my wife.

Realizing others might also benefit from a Website with this kind of factual information, www.largedividends.com was launched on September 1999.

The successful mutual fund reports_are presented for informational purposes only. There is no guarantee of completeness and accuracy. Mutual fund performance and returns are based on the last End-of-Year market closing.

Further, the reports are not offered to buy or sell a particular fund. All of the listed mutual funds are open to all investors. There is no guarantee of future results. Always contact the mutual fund and read the prospectus before making any investment

Current returns of the 32 mutual funds are posted weekly on, Mutual Interest Data, Ltd. website, www.largedividends.com

Convertible Securities (CS)
Fidelity Convertible A – FCVSX
800-544-8544

Fidelity Investments
82 Devonshire St.
Boston, MA 02109

Net Asset Value: $32.59
Dividend Distribution: $.10
Total Return 4/10/15: 1.43%
Risk: High
Minimum Investment Purchase: $2500
Minimum IRA Purchase: $2500
Maximum Front End Sales Load: None
Date of Inception: January 5, 1987
Number of Years of Gains: 22
Number of Years of Losses: 5
Net Expense Ratio: 0.72%
Category Average Net Expense Ratio: 1.15%

FIVE YEAR ANNUAL RETURNS

Year: 2014
2013 Net Asset Value: $31.11
Dividend Distribution: $1.76   (5.66%)
2014 Net Asset Value: $32.23
Performance: 3.60%
Category Rank: 12%
Total Return: 9.26%

Year: 2013
2012 Net Asset Value: $25.91
Dividend Distribution: $1.03   (3.99%)
2013 Net Asset Value: $31.11   (20.07%)
Total Return: 24.06%

Year: 2012
2011 Net Asset Value: $22.83
Dividend Distribution: $.76   (3.33%)
2012 Net Asset Value: $25.91   (13.49%)
Total Return: 16.82%

Year: 2011
2010 Net Asset Value: $25.45
Dividend Distribution: $.75   (2.96%)
2011 Net Asset Value: $22.83   (-10.29%)
Total Return: -7.33%

Year: 2010
2009 Net Asset Value: $21.80
Dividend Distribution: $.90   (4.11%)
2010 Net Asset Value: $25.45   (16.74%)
Total Return: 20.85%

Averages	Dividends	Performance	Total Return
Five years	4.01%	8.72%	12.73%
Three years	4.33%	12.39%	16.71%
Two years	4.82%	11.83%	16.66%

Emerging Markets (EM)
Van Eck Emerging Markets -GBFAX
800-826-1115

Van Eck Funds
335 Madison Avenue, 19th Floor
New York, NY 10017

Net Asset Value $15.38
Dividend Distribution: $0.00
Total Return 4/10/15: 8.01%
Risk: High
Minimum Investment Purchase: $1,000
Minimum IRA Purchase: N/A
Maximum Front End Sales Load: 5.75%
Date of Inception: December 20. 1993
Number of Years of Gains: 14
Number of Years of Losses: 7
Net Expense Ratio: 1.63%
Category Average Net Expense Ratio: 1.56%

FIVE YEAR ANNUAL RETURNS:

Year: 2014
2013 Net Asset Value: $14.34
Dividend Distribution: $0.00   (0.00%)
2014 Net Asset Value: $14.24
Performance: -0.70%
Category Rank: 30%
Total Return: -0.70%

Year: 2013
2012 Net Asset Value: $12.94
Dividend Distribution: $.06   (0.49%)
2013 Net Asset Value: $14.34   (10.82%)
Total Return: 11.31%

Year: 2012
2011 Net Asset Value: $9.92
Dividend Distribution: $.00   (0.00%)
2012 Net Asset Value: $12.94   (30.44%)
Total Return: 30.44%

Year: 2011
2010 Net Asset Value: $13.69
Dividend Distribution: $.13   (0.96%)
2011 Net Asset Value: $9.92   (−27.54%)
Total Return: -26.58%

Year: 2010
2009 Net Asset Value: $10.71
Dividend Distribution: $.04   (0.35%)
2010 Net Asset Value: $13.69   (27.82%)
Total Return: 28.17%

Averages	Dividends	Performance	Total Return
Five years	0.36%	8.17%	8.53%
Three years	0.16%	13.52%	13.68%
Two years	0.24%	5.06%	5.30%

Equity Income (EI)
Pioneer Equity Income A – PEQIX
800-225-6292

Pioneer Investments
60 State Street
Boston, MA 02109

Net Asset Value: $34.92
Dividend Distribution: $.14
Total Return 4/10/15: 2.04%
Risk: Below Average
Minimum Investment Purchase: $1000
Minimum IRA Purchase: $250
Maximum Front End Sales Load: 5.75%
Date of Inception: July 25, 1990
Number of Years of Gains: 20
Number of Years of Losses: 4
Net Expense Ratio: 1.10%
Category Average Net Expense Ratio: 1.13%

FIVE YEAR ANNUAL RETURNS:

Year: 2014
2013 Net Asset Value: $34.13
Dividend Distribution: $4.15   (12.15%)
2014 Net Asset Value: $34.36
Performance: 0.67%
Category Rank: Top 15%
Total Return: 12.82%

Year: 2013
2012 Net Asset Value: $28.76
Dividend Distribution: $2.94 (10.22%)
2013 Net Asset Value: $34.13 (18.67%)
Total Return: 28.89%

Year: 2012
2011 Net Asset Value: $26.44
Dividend Distribution: $1.03 (3.89%)
2012 Net Asset Value: $28.76 (8.77%)
Total Return: 12.67%

Year: 2011
2010 Net Asset Value: $25.35
Dividend Distribution: $.57 (2.25%)
2011 Net Asset Value: $26.44 (4.30%)
Total Return: 6.55%

Year: 2010
2009 Net Asset Value: $21.64
Dividend Distribution: $.44 (2.02%)
2010 Net Asset Value: $25.35 (17.14%)
Total Return: 19.16%

Averages	Dividends	Performance	Total Return
Five years	6.10%	9.91%	16.01%
Three years	8.75%	9.37%	18.13%
Two years	11.19%	9.67%	20.86%

Flexible Portfolio (FP)
Bruce Fund – BRUFX
800-872-7823

Bruce and Company
20 North Wacker Drive. – Suite 2414
Chicago, IL 60606

Net Asset Value: $521.54
Dividend Distribution: $0.00
Total Return 4/10/15: 3.30%
Risk: Above Average
Minimum Investment Purchase: $1000
Minimum IRA Purchase: N/A
Maximum Front End Sales Load: None
Date of Inception: October 17, 1983
Number of Years of Gains: 23
Number of Years of Losses: 8
Net Expense Ratio: 0.70%
Category Average Net Expense Ratio: 0.93%

FIVE YEAR ANNUAL RETURNS:

Year: 2014
2013 Net Asset Value: $457.83
Dividend Distribution: $15.89   (3.47%)
2014 Net Asset Value: $504.88
Performance: 10.28%
Category Rank: Top 4%
Total Return: 13.75%

Year: 2013
2012 Net Asset Value: $394.74
Dividend Distribution: $11.43   (2.90%)
2013 Net Asset Value: $457.83   (15.98%)
Total Return: 18.88%

Year: 2012
2011 Net Asset Value: $379.67
Dividend Distribution: $14.76   (3.89%)
2012 Net Asset Value: $394.74   (3.97%)
Total Return: 7.86%

Year: 2011
2010 Net Asset Value: $367.77
Dividend Distribution: $14.71   (4.00%)
2011 Net Asset Value: $379.67   (3.24%)
Total Return: 7.24%

Year: 2010
2009 Net Asset Value: $309.66
Dividend Distribution: $15.84   (5.12%)
2019 Net Asset Value: $367.77   (18.77%)
Total Return: 23.89%

Averages	Dividends	Performance	Total Return
Five years	3.87%	10.45%	14.32%
Three years	3.42%	10.08%	13.49%
Two years	3.18%	13.13%	13.13%

Global Growth (GL)
Franklin/Templeton Growth A TEPLX
800-632-2301

Franklin Templeton Funds
500 East Broward Blvd – Suite 2100
Fort Lauderdale, FL 33394-3091

Net Asset Value: $24.84
Dividend Distribution: $0.00
Total Return: 4.33%
Risk: Above Average
Minimum Investment Purchase: $1000
Minimum IRA Purchase: $250
Maximum Front End Sales Load: 5.75%
Date of Inception: November 29, 1954
Number of Years of Gains: 47
Number of Years of Losses: 13
Net Expense Ratio: 1.03%
Category Average Net Expense Ratio: 1.33%

FIVE YEAR ANNUAL RETURNS:

Year: 2014
2013 Net Asset Value: $24.97
Dividend Distribution: $.68   (2.74%)
2014 Net Asset Value: $23.81
Performance: -4.65%
Category Rank: 79%
Total Return: -1.91%

Year: 2013
2012 Net Asset Value: $19.91
Dividend Distribution: $.94   (4.74%)
2013 Net Asset Value: $24.97   (25.41%)
Total Return: 30.15%

Year: 2012
2011 Net Asset Value: $16.29
Dividend Distribution: $.36   (2.24%)
2012 Net Asset Value: $19.91   (22.22%)
Total Return: 24.46%

Year: 2011
2010 Net Asset Value: $17.79
Dividend Distribution: $.36   (2.05%)
2011 Net Asset Value: $16.29   (-8.43%)
Total Return: -6.38%

Year: 2010
2009 Net Asset Value: $16.81
Dividend Distribution: $.29   (1.71%)
2010 Net Asset Value: $17.79   (5.83%)
Total Return: 7.54%

Averages	Dividends	Performance	Total Return
Five years	2.69%	8.08%	10.77%
Three years	3.24%	14.33%	17.57%
Two years	3.74%	10.38%	14.12%

Health/Bio-Tech (HB)
Vanguard Health Care – VGHCX
800-662-7447

Vanguard Group
P.O. Box 2600 – V26
Valley forge, PA 19482

Net Asset Value: $230.75
Dividend Distribution: $6.42
Total Return 4/10/15: 12.10%
Risk: Above Average
Minimum Investment Purchase: $3000
Minimum IRA Purchase: $3000
Maximum Front End Sales Load: None
Date of Inception: May 23, 1984
Number of Years of Gains: 25
Number of Years of Losses: 5
Net Expense Ratio: 0.35%
Category Average Net Expense Ratio: 1.43%

FIVE YEAR ANNUAL RETURNS:

Year: 2014
2013 Net Asset Value: $187.16
Dividend Distribution: $28.82   (15.40%)
2014 Net Asset Value: $211.71
Category Rank: Top 20%
Total Return: 28.52%

Year: 2013
2012 Net Asset Value: $143.27
Dividend Distribution: $17.99   (12.56%)
2013 Net Asset Value: $187.16   (30.63%)
Total Return: 43.19%

Year: 2012
2011 Net Asset Value: $128.73
Dividend Distribution: $4.92   (3.82%)
2012 Net Asset Value: $143.27   (11.29%)
Total Return: 15.11%

Year: 2011
2010 Net Asset Value: $122.40
Dividend Distribution: $7.69   (6.28%)
2011 Net Asset Value: $128.73   (5.17%)
Total Return: 11.45%

Year: 2010
2009 Net Asset Value: $120.22
Dividend Distribution: $5.20   (4.33%)
2010 Net Asset Value: $122.40   (1.81%)
Total Return: 6.14%

Averages	Dividends	Performance	Total Return
Five years	8.48%	12.41%	20.88%
Three years	10.59%	18.35%	28.94%
Two years	13.98%	21.88%	35.85%

International Large Value (INTL)
Putnam Intl Value A - PNGAX
800-225-1581

Putnam Funds
One Post Office Square
Boston, MA 02109

Net Asset Value: $11.19
Dividend Distribution: $0.00
Total Return 4/10/15: 7.80%
Risk: Above Average
Minimum Investment Purchase: $500
Minimum IRA Purchase: N/A
Maximum Front End Sales Load: 5.75%
Date of Inception: August 1, 1996
Number of Years of Gains: 13
Number of Years of Losses: 5
Net Expense Ratio: 1.34%
Category Average Net Expense Ratio: 1.30%

FIVE YEAR ANNUAL RETURNS:

Year: 2014
2013 Net Asset Value: $11.74
Dividend Distribution: $.21   (1.75%)
2014 Net Asset Value: $10.38
Performance: -11.58%
Category Rank: 72%
Total Return: -9.83%

Year: 2013
2012 Net Asset Value: $9.75
Dividend Distribution: $.16 (1.63%)
2013 Net Asset Value: $11.74 (20.41%)
Total Return: 22.04%

Year: 2012
2011 Net Asset Value: $8.13
Dividend Distribution: $.13 (1.56%)
2012 Net Asset Value: $9.75 (19.93%)
Total Return: 21.49%

Year: 2011
2010 Net Asset Value: $9.94
Dividend Distribution: $.47 (4.68%)
2011 Net Asset Value: $8.13 (-18.21%)
Total Return: -13.53%

Year: 2010
2009 Net Asset Value: $9.39
Dividend Distribution: $.13 ($1.43)
2010 Net Asset Value: $9.94 (5.86%
Total Return: 7.29%

Averages	Dividends	Performance	Total Return
Five years	2.21%	3.28%	5.49%
Three years	1.65%	9.58%	11.23%
Two years	1.69%	4.41%	6.10%

Large–Cap Core (LC)
Oakmark I - OAKMX
800–625–6275

Harris Associates LPT
Two N. LaSalle Street - Suite 500
Chicago, IL 60602–3790

Net Asset Value: $67.52
Dividend Distribution: $0.00
Total Return 4/10/15: 1.72%
Risk: Above Average
Minimum Investment Purchase: $1000
Minimum IRA Purchase: $1000
Maximum Front End Sales Load: None
Date of Inception: August 5, 1991
Number of Years of Gains: 18
Number of Years of Losses: 5
Net Expense Ratio: 0.87%
Category Average Net Expense Ratio: 1.09%

FIVE YEAR ANNUAL RETURNS:

Year: 2014
2013 Net Asset Value: $63.63
Dividend Distribution: $4.57   (7.19%)
2014 Net Asset Value: $66.38
Performance: 4.32%
Category Rank: 49%
Total Return: 11.51%

Year: 2013

2012 Net Asset Value: $48.53
Dividend Distribution: $3.00 (6.18%)
2013 Net Asset Value: $63.63 (31.11%)
Total Return: 37.29%

Year: 2012

2011 Net Asset Value: $41.69
Dividend Distribution: $1.88 (4.15%
2012 Net Asset Value: $48.53 (16.41%)
Total Return: 20.91%

Year: 2011

2010 Net Asset Value: $41.30
Dividend Distribution: $.36 (0.88%)
2011 Net Asset Value: $41.69 (0.94%)
Total Return: 1.82%

Year: 2010

2009 Net Asset Value: $37.04
Dividend Distribution: $.25 (0.68%)
2010 Net Asset Value: $41.30 (11.50%)
Total Return: 12.18%

Averages	Dividends	Performance	Total Return
Five years	3.89%	12.86%	16.74%
Three years	5.96%	17.28%	23.24%
Two years	6.68%	17.72%	24.40%

Large–Cap Growth (LG)
Elfun Trusts - ELFNX
800-242-0134

Elfun Diversified Fund
3001 Summer St.
Stamford, CT 06905

Net Asset Value: $60.11
Dividend Distribution: $0.00
Total Return 4/10/15: 3.60%
Risk: Average
Minimum Investment Purchase: $500
Minimum IRA Purchase: $500
Maximum Front End Sales Load: None
Date of Inception: May 27, 1935
Number of Years of Gains: 27
Number of Years of Losses: 4
Net Expense Ratio: 0.15%
Category Average Net Expense Ratio: 1.20%

FIVE YEAR ANNUAL RETURNS:

Year 2014
2013 Net Asset Value: $56.07
Dividend Distribution: $5.41   (9.65%)
2014 Net Asset Value: $58.02
Performance: 3.48%
Category Rank: Top 22%
Total Return: 13.13%

Year: 2013
2012 Net Asset Value: $44.06
Dividend Distribution: $3.40   (7.72%)
2013 Net Asset Value: $56.07   (27.26%)
Total Return: 34.98%

Year: 2012
2011 Net Asset Value: $40.35
Dividend Distribution: $4.84   (11.98%
2012 Net Asset Value: $44.06   (9.19%)
Total Return: 21.18%

Year: 2011
2010 Net Asset Value: $41.38
Dividend Distribution: $1.58   (3.82%)
2011 Net Asset Value: $40.35   (-2.49%)
Total Return: 1.33%

Year: 2010
2009 Net Asset Value: $38.50
Dividend Distribution: $2.15   (5.59%)
2010 Net Asset Value: $41.38   (7.48%)
Total Return: 13.07%

Averages	Dividends	Performance	Total Return
Five years	7.75%	8.98%	16.74%
Three years	9.78%	13.31%	23.09%
Two years	8.68%	15.37%	24.05%

Large–Cap Value (LV)
T. Rowe Price Value - TRVLX
800-638-5660

T. Rowe Price Funds
100 E. Pratt St.
Baltimore, MD 21202

Net Asset Value: $35.68
Dividend Distribution: $0.00
Total Return 4/10/15: 2.97%
Risk: Above Average
Minimum Investment Purchase: $2500
Minimum IRA Purchase: $1000
Maximum Front End Sales Load: None
Date of Inception: September 30, 1994
Number of Years of Gains: 17
Number of Years of Losses: 3
Net Expense Ratio: 0.84%
Category Average Net Expense Ratio: 1.13%

FIVE YEAR ANNUAL RETURNS:

Year 2014
2013 Net Asset Value: $33.77
Dividend Distribution: $3.63   (10.76%)
2014 Net Asset Value: $34.65
Performance: 2.61%
Category Rank: Top 9%
Total Return: 13.37%

Year: 2013
2012 Net Asset Value: $26.38
Dividend Distribution: $2.45   (9.30%)
2013 Net Asset Value: $33.77   (28.01%
Total Return: 37.31%

Year: 2012
2011 Net Asset Value: $22.54
Dividend Distribution: $.54   (2.40%)
2012 Net Asset Value: $26.38   (17.04%
Total Return: 19.44%

Year: 2011
2010 Net Asset Value: $23.34
Dividend Distribution: $.32   (1.37%)
2011 Net Asset Value: $22.54   (-3.43%)
Total Return: -2.06%

Year: 2010
2009 Net Asset Value: $20.48
Dividend Distribution: $.41   (2.00%)
2010 Net Asset Value: $23.34   (13.96%)
Total Return: 15.96%

Averages	Dividends	Performance	Total Return
Five years	5.17%	11.64%	16.80%
Three years	7.48%	23.37%	23.37%
Two years	10.03%	15.31%	25.34%

Mid-Cap Core (MC)
Ariel Investor - ARGFX
800-292-7435

Ariel Investor
200 East Randolph Drive- Suite 2900
Chicago IL 60601

Net Asset Value: $77.21
Dividend Distribution: $0.00
Total Return 4/10/15: 7.50%
Risk: High
Minimum Investment Purchase: $1000
Minimum IRA Purchase: $1000
Maximum Front End Sales Load: None
Date of Inception: November 6, 1986
Number of Years of Gains: 21
Number of Years of Losses: 7
Net Expense Ratio: 1.03%
Category Average Net Expense Ratio: 1.19%

FIVE YEAR ANNUAL RETURNS:

Year 2014
2013 Net Asset Value: $73.68
Dividend Distribution: $9.93   (13.47%)
2014 Net Asset Value: $71.82
Performance: -2.52%
Category Rank: 26%
Total Return: 10.95%

Year: 2013
2012 Net Asset Value: $51.21
Dividend Distribution: $.41   (0.80%)
2013 Net Asset Value: $73.68   (43.88%)
Total Return: 44.68%

Year: 2012
2011 Net Asset Value: $42.97
Dividend Distribution: $.49   (1.14%)
2012 Net Asset Value: $51.21   (19.18%)
Total Return: 20.32%

Year: 2011
2010 Net Asset Value: $48.57
Dividend Distribution: $.09   (0.19%)
2011 Net Asset Value: $42.97   (-11.53%)
Total Return: -11.34%

Year: 2010
2009 Net Asset Value: $38.56
Dividend Distribution: $.01   (.01%)
2010 Net Asset Value: $48.57   (25.96%)
Total Return: 25.97%

Averages	Dividends	Performance	Total Return
Five years	3.12%	14.99%	18.11%
Three years	5.14%	20.18%	25.31%
Two years	7.13%	20.68%	27.81%

Mid–Cap Growth (MG)
Goldman Sachs Growth Oppty -GGOAX
800-526-7384

Goldman Sachs Trust
200 West Street
New York, NY 10282

Net Asset Value: $25.97
Dividend Distribution: $0.00
Total Return 4/10/15: 4.59%
Risk: Average
Minimum Investment Purchase: $1000
Minimum IRA Purchase: $250
Maximum Front End Sales Load: 5.50%
Date of Inception: May 24, 1999
Number of Years of Gains: 12
Number of Years of Losses: 3
Net Expense Ratio: 1.36%
Category Average Net Expense Ratio: 1.33%

FIVE YEAR ANNUAL RETURNS:

Year: 2014
2013 Net Asset Value: $27.94
Dividend Distribution: $6.18   (22.12%)
2014 Net Asset Value: $24.83
Performance: -11.13%
Category Rank: Top 18%
Total Return: 10.99%

Year: 2013
2012 Net Asset Value: $22.91
Dividend Distribution: $2.26   (9.86%)
2013 Net Asset Value: $27.94   (21.96%)
Total Return: 31.82%

Year: 2012
2011 Net Asset Value: $20.66
Dividend Distribution: $1.65   (7.98%)
2012 Net Asset Value: $22.91   (10.89%)
Total Return: 18.87%

Year: 2011
2010 Net Asset Value: $22.96
Dividend Distribution: $1.39   (6.06%)
2011 Net Asset Value: $20.66   (-10.02)
Total Return: -3.96%

Year: 2010
2009 Net Asset Value: $19.54
Dividend Distribution: $.22   (1.13%)
2010 Net Asset Value: $22.96   (17.15%)
Total Return: 18.63%

Averages	Dividends	Performance	Total Return
Five years	9.43%	5.84%	15.27%
Three years	13.32%	7.24%	20.56%
Two years	15.99%	5.41%	21.40%

Mid-Cap Value (MV)
Columbia Mid-Cap Value A - NAMAX
800-345-6611

Columbia Funds Series Trust
1 Financial Center
Boston, MA 02111

Net Asset Value: $17.41
Dividend Distribution: $.02
Total Return 4/10/15: 2.23%
Risk: Average
Minimum Investment Purchase: $2000
Minimum IRA Purchase: $1000
Maximum Front End Sales Load: None
Date of Inception: November 20, 2001
Number of Years of Gains: 10
Number of Years of Losses: 3
Net Expense Ratio: 0.92%
Category Average Net Expense Ratio: 1.24%

FIVE YEAR ANNUAL RETURNS:

Year: 2014
2013 Net Asset Value: $17.91
Dividend Distribution: $3.07   (17.12%)
2014 Net Asset Value: $17.05
Performance: -4.80%
Category Rank: Top 15%
Total Return: 12.32%

Year: 2013
2012 Net Asset Value: $14.82
Dividend Distribution: $2.16   (14.59%)
2013 Net Asset Value: $17.91   (20.85%)
Total Return: 35.44%

Year: 2012
2011 Net Asset Value: $12.87
Dividend Distribution: $.15   (1.15%)
2012 Net Asset Value: $14.82   (15.69%)
Total Return: 16.84%

Year: 2011
2010 Net Asset Value: $13.46
Dividend Distribution: $.11   (0.80%)
2011 Net Asset Value: $12.81   (-4.83%)
Total Return: -4.03%

Year: 2010
2009 Net Asset Value: $11.08
Dividend Distribution: $.19   (1.73%)
2010 Net Asset Value: $13.46   (21.48%)
Total Return: 23.21%

Averages	Dividends	Performance	Total Return
Five years	7.08%	9.68%	16.76%
Three years	10.95%	10.58%	21.53%
Two years	15.85%	8.02%	23.88%

Mixed-Asset Target Allocation: Conservative (MAC)
Vanguard Wellesley Income- VWINX
800-662-7447

Vanguard Group
P. O. Box 2600 – V 26
Valley Forge PA 19482

Net Asset Value: $25.91
Dividend Distribution: $.17
Total Return 4/10/15: 2.01%
Risk: Average
Minimum Investment Purchase: $3000
Minimum IRA Purchase: $3000
Maximum Front End Sales Load: None
Date of Inception: July 1, 1970
Number of Years of Gains: 38
Number of Years of Losses: 6
Net Expense Ratio: 0.25%
Category Average Net Expense Ratio: 0.83%

FIVE YEAR ANNUAL RETURNS:

Year: 2014
2013 Net Asset Value: $24.85
Dividend Distribution: $1.28   (5.17%)
2014 Net Asset Value: $25.57
Performance: 2.90%
Category Rank: Top 9%
Total Return: 8.07%

Year: 2013
2012 Net Asset Value: $24.11
Dividend Distribution: $1.48   (6.12%)
2013 Net Asset Value: $24.85   (3.07%)
Total Return: 9.19%

Year: 2012
2011 Net Asset Value: $22.93
Dividend Distribution: $1.13   (4.91%)
2012 Net Asset Value: $24.11   (5.15%)
Total Return: 10.06%

Year: 2011
2010 Net Asset Value: $21.70
Dividend Distribution: $.86   (3.96%)
2011 Net Asset Value: $22.93   (5.67%)
Total Return: 9.63%

Year: 2010
2009 Net Asset Value: $20.37
Dividend Distribution: $.84   (4.12%)
2010 Net Asset Value: $21.70   (6.53%)
Total Return: 10.65%

Averages	Dividends	Performance	Total Return
Five years	4.86%	4.66%	9.52%
Three years	5.40%	3.70%	9.11%
Two years	5.65%	5.65%	8.63%

Mixed-Asset Targeted Allocation: Growth (MAG)
Tributary Balanced Fund - FOBAX
800-662-4203

Tributary funds, Inc.
P. O. Box 219022
Kansas City MO 64141 – 6022

Net Asset Value: $17.79
Dividend Distribution: $.01
Total Return 4/10/15: 5.96%
Risk: Average
Minimum Investment Purchase: $1000
Minimum IRA Purchase: N/A
Maximum Front End Sales Load: None
Date of Inception: August 6, 1996
Number of Years of Gains: 15
Number of Years of Losses: 3
Net Expense Ratio: 1.16%
Category Average Net Expense Ratio: 0.93%

FIVE YEAR ANNUAL RETURNS:

Year: 2014
2013 Net Asset Value: $17.34
Dividend Distribution: $1.56   (8.98%)
2014 Net Asset Value: $16.79
Performance: -3.17%
Category Rank: 55%
Total Return: 5.81%

Year: 2013
2012 Net Asset Value: $15.34
Dividend Distribution: $1.36   (8.86%)
2013 Net Asset Value: $17.34   (13.04%)
Total Return: 21.90%

Year: 2012
2011 Net Asset Value: $14.18
Dividend Distribution: $.14   (0.98%)
2012 Net Asset Value: $15.34   (8.18%)
Total Return: 9.16%

Year: 2011
2010 Net Asset Value: $13.55
Dividend Distribution: $.15   (1.09%)
2011 Net Asset Value: $14.18   (4.65%)
Total Return: 5.74%

Year: 2010
2009 Net Asset Value : $11.72
Dividend Distribution: $.23   (1.95%)
2010 Net Asset Value: $13.55   (15.61%)
Total Return: 17.56%

Averages	Dividends	Performance	Total Return
Five years	4.37%	7.66%	12.03%
Three years	6.27%	6.02%	12.29%
Two years	8.92%	4.93%	13.85%

Mixed–Asset Target Allocation:
Moderate (MAM)
Buffalo Flexible Income – BUFBX
800-225-6292

Buffalo Funds
P.O. Box 701
Milwaukee, WI 53201

Net Asset Value: $14.70
Dividend Distribution: $.07
Total Return 4/10/15: 2.04%
Risk: Above Average
Minimum Investment Purchase: $2500
Minimum IRA Purchase: $250
Maximum Front End Sales Load: None
Date of Inception: August 12, 1994
Number of Years of Gains: 17
Number of Years of Losses: 3
Net Expense Ratio: 1.01%
Category Average Net Expense Ratio: 0.96%

FIVE YEAR ANNUAL RETURNS:

Year: 2014
2013 Net Asset Value: $14.30
Dividend Distribution: $.33   (2.33%)
2014 Net Asset Value: $14.48
Performance: 1.26%
Category Rank: 75%
Total Return: 3.59%

Year: 2013
2012 Net Asset Value: $12.67
Dividend Distribution: $.48   (3.81%)
2013 Net Asset Value: $14.30   (12.87%)
Total Return: 14.68%

Year: 2012
2011 Net Asset Value: $11.83
Dividend Distribution: $.38   (3.20%)
2012 Net Asset Value: $12.67   (7.10%)
Total Return: 10.30%

Year: 2011
2010 Net Asset Value: $11.14
Dividend Distribution: $.38   (3.44%)
2011 Net Asset Value: $11.83   (6.19%)
Total Return: 9.63%

Year: 2010
2009 Net Asset Value: $10.28
Dividend Distribution: $.34   (3.31%)
2010 Net Asset Value: $11.14   (8.37%)
Total Return: 11.68%

Averages	Dividends	Performance	Total Return
Five years	3.22%	7.16%	10.38%
Three years	3.11%	7.07%	10.19%
Two years	3.07%	7.06%	10.13%

Multi-Cap Core (MUC)
Olstein All Cap Value–OFAFX
800-799-2113

Olstein All Cap Value
4 Manhattanville Rd
Purchase NY 10577

Net Asset Value: $25.80
Dividend Distribution: $0.00
Total Return for 4/10/15: 3.41%
Risk: High
Minimum Investment Purchase: $1000
Minimum IRA Purchase: $1000
Maximum Front End Sales Load: None
Date of Inception: September 20, 1999
Number of Years of Gains: 11
Number of Years of Losses: 4
Net Expense Ratio: 1.34%
Category Average Net Expense Ratio: 1.09%

FIVE YEAR ANNUAL RETURNS:

Year: 2014
2013 Net Asset Value: $21.79
Dividend Distribution: $0.00   (0.00%)
2014 Net Asset Value: $24.95
Performance: 14.50%
Category Rank: Top 3%
Total Return: 14.15%

Year: 2013
2012 Net Asset Value: $15.77
 Dividend Distribution: $.16   (1.00%)
2013 Net Asset Value: $21.79   (38.17%)
Total Return: 39.17%

Year: 2012
2011 Net Asset Value: $13.58
Dividend Distribution: $.00   (0.00%)
2012 Net Asset Value: $15.77   (16.13%)
Total Return: 16.13%

Year: 2011
2010 Net Asset Value: $14.08
Dividend Distribution: $.00   (0.00%)
2011 Net Asset Value: $13.58   (-3.55%)
Total Return: -3.55%

Year: 2010
2009 Net Asset Value: $12.03
Dividend Distribution: $.00   (0.00%)
2010 Net Asset Value: $14.08   (17.04%)
Total Return: 17.04%

Averages	Dividends	Performance	Total Return
Five years	0.20%	16.46%	16.66%
Three years	0.33%	22.93%	23.27%
Two years	0.50%	26.34%	26.84%

Multi–Cap Growth (MUG)
Federated Kaufmann a – KAUAX
800–341–7400

Federated Kaufmann A
Federated Investors Tower
Pittsburgh PA 15222 – 3779

Net Asset Value: $6.44
Dividend Distribution: $0.00
Total Return 4/10/15: 11.61%
Risk: Below Average
Minimum Investment Purchase: $1500
Minimum IRA Purchase: $250
Maximum Front End Sales Load: 5.50%
Date of Inception: April 24, 2001
Number of Years of Gains: 10
Number of Years of Losses: 3
Net Expense Ratio: 1.95%
Category Average Net Expense Ratio: 1.30%

FIVE YEAR ANNUAL RETURNS:

Year: 2014
2013 Net Asset Value: $6.16
Dividend Distribution: $.95   (15.48%)
2014 Net Asset Value: $5.77
Performance: -6.33%
Category Rank: 49%
Total Return: 9.15%

Year: 2013
2012 Net Asset Value: $5.02
Dividend Distribution: $.89   (17.65%)
2013 Net Asset Value: $6.16   (22.71%)
 Total Return: 40.36%

Year: 2012
2011 Net Asset Value: $4.65
Dividend Distribution: $.43   (9.35%)
2012 Net Asset Value: $5.02   (7.96%)
Total Return: 17.31%

Year: 2011
2010 Net Asset Value: $5.49
Dividend Distribution: $.09   (1.68%)
2011 Net Asset Value: $4.65   (-15.30%)
Total Return: -13.62%

Year: 2010
2009 Net Asset Value: $4.66
Dividend Distribution: $.03   (0.73%)
2010 Net Asset Value: $5.49   (17.81%)
Total Return: 18.54%

Averages	Dividends	Performance	Total Return
Five years	8.98%	5.37%	14.35%
Three years	14.16%	8.11%	22.27%
Two years	16.57%	8.19%	24.76%

Multi–Cap Value (MUV)
Hotchkis & Wiley Value Opps A HWAAX
866-493-8637

Hotchkis & Wiley Value Opportunities A
725 S. Figuera Street - 39th floor
Los Angeles, CA 90017–5439

Net Asset Value: $28.82
Dividend Distribution: $0.00
Total Return 4/10/15: 3.78%
Risk: Above Average
Minimum Investment Purchase: $2500
Minimum IRA Purchase: $250
Maximum Front End Sales Load: None
Date of Inception: December 31, 2002
Number of Years of Gains: 9
Number of Years of Losses: 3
Net Expense Ratio: 1.24%
Category Average Net Expense Ratio: 1.24%

FIVE YEAR ANNUAL RETURNS:

Year: 2014
2013 Net Asset Value: $27.63
Dividend Distribution: $2.57   (9.29%)
2014 Net Asset Value: $27.77
Performance: 0.51%
Category Rank: 35%
Total Return: 9.80%

Year: 2013
2012 Net Asset Value: $21.49
Dividend Distribution: $1.90   (8.85%)
2013 Net Asset Value: $27.63   (28.57)
Total Return: 37.42%

Year: 2012
2011 Net Asset Value: $17.62
Dividend Distribution: $1.26   (7.17%)
2012 Net Asset Value: $21.49   (21.96%)
Total Return: 29.14%

Year: 2011
2010 Net Asset Value: $19.54
Dividend Distribution: $.83   (4.25%)
2011 Net Asset Value: $17.62   (-9.83%)
Total Return: -5.58%

Year: 2010
2009 Net Asset Value: $14.67
Dividend Distribution: $.20   (1.34%)
2010 Net Asset Value: $19.54   (33.20%)
Total Return: 34.53%

Averages	Dividends	Performance	Total Return
Five years	6.18%	14.88%	21.06%
Three years	8.44%	25.45%	25.45%
Two years	9.07%	14.54%	23.61%

Small–Cap Core (SC)
MassMutual Premier Small-Cap Opps - DLBMX
888-309-3539

Mass. Mutual Premier Small–Cap A
1295 State Street
Springfield, MA 01111

Net Asset Value: $15.33
Dividend Distribution: $0.00
Total Return 4/10//15: 3.44%
Risk: Above Average
Minimum Investment Purchase: N/A
Minimum IRA Purchase: N/A
Maximum Front End Sales Load: 5.75%
Date of Inception: July 17, 1998
Number of Years of Gains: 11
Number of Years of Losses: 5
Net Expense Ratio: 1.15%
Category Average Net Expense Ratio: 1.26%

FIVE YEAR ANNUAL RETURNS:

Year: 2014
2013 Net Asset Value: $15.50
Dividend Distribution: $2.48   (15.99%)
2014 Net Asset Value: $14.82
Performance: -4.39%
Category Rank: Top 3%
Total Return: 11.60%

Year: 2013
2012 Net Asset Value: $11.10
Dividend Distribution: $.10   (0.86%)
2013 Net Asset Value: $15.50   (39.64%)
Total Return: 40.50%

Year: 2012
2011 Net Asset Value: $9.49
Dividend Distribution: $.34   (3.58%)
2012 Net Asset Value: $11.10   (16.97%)
Total Return: 20.55%

Year: 2011
2010 Net Asset Value: $9.76
Dividend Distribution: $.02   (0.23%)
2011 Net Asset Value: $9.49   (-2.77%)
Total Return: -2.54%

Year: 2010
2009 Net Asset Value: $7.94
Dividend Distribution: $.03   (0.36%)
2010 Net Asset Value: $9.76   (22.92%)
Total Return: 23.28%

Averages	Dividends	Performance	Total Return
Five years	4.20%	14.47%	18.68%
Three years	6.81%	17.41%	24.22%
Two years	8.42%	17.63%	26.05%

Small-Cap Growth (SG)
Janus Venture T - JAVTX
800-525-0020

Janus Investment Fund
151 Detroit Street
Denver CO 80206

Net Asset Value: $68.75
Dividend Distribution: $0.00
Total Return: 5.75%
Risk: Average
Minimum Investment Purchase: $2500
Minimum IRA Purchase: N/A
Maximum Front End Sales Load: None
Date of Inception: April 30, 1985
Number of Years of Gains: 24
Number of Years of Losses: 5
Net Expense Ratio: 0.94%
Category Average Net Expense Ratio: 1.38%

FIVE YEAR ANNUAL RETURNS:

Year: 2014
2013 Net Asset Value: $65.56
Dividend Distribution: $7.24   (11.05%)
2013 Net Asset Value: $65.01
Performance: -.84%
Category Rank: Top 4%
Total Return: 10.21%

Year: 2013
2012 Net Asset Value: $54.33
Dividend Distribution: $11.45   (21.07%)
2013 Net Asset Value: $65.56   (20.67%)
Total Return: 41.74%

Year: 2012
2011 Net Asset Value: $52.15
Dividend Distribution: $6.65   (12.76%)
2012 Net Asset Value: $54.33   (4.18%)
Total Return: 16.94%

Year: 2011
2010 Net Asset Value: $55.10
Dividend Distribution: $4.08   (7.40%)
2011 Net Asset Value: $52.15   (-5.35%)
Total Return: 2.04%

Year: 2010
2009 Net Asset Value: $43.40
Dividend Distribution: $.00   (0.00%)
2010 Net Asset Value: $55.10   (26.96%)
Total Return: 26.96%

Averages	Dividends	Performance	Total Return
Five years	10.45%	9.12%	19.58%
Three years	14.96%	8.00%	22.96%
Two years	16.06%	9.92%	25.98%

Small-Cap Value (SV)
Hotchkis & Wiley SC Value A HWSAX
866-493-8637

Hotchkis & Wiley Small Cap Value A
725 South Figueroa Street 39th Floor
Los Angeles CA 90017-5439

Net Asset Value: $61.92
Dividend Distribution: $0.00
Total Return 4/10/15: 2.72%
Risk: Above Average
Minimum Investment Purchase: $2500
Minimum IRA Purchase: $1000
Maximum Front End Sales Load: 5.25%
Date of Inception: October 6, 2000
Number of Years of Gains: 10
Number of Years of Losses: 4
Net Expense Ratio: 1.24%
Category Average Net Expense Ratio: 1.33%

FIVE YEAR ANNUAL RETURNS:

Year: 2014
2013 Net Asset Value: $61.21
Dividend Distribution: $7.76   (12.68%)
2014 Net Asset Value: $60.28
Performance: -1.52%
Category Rank: Top 2%
Total Return: 11.16%

Year: 2013
2012 Net Asset Value: $45.69
Dividend Distribution: $5.48 (12.00%)
2013 Net Asset Value: $61.21 (33.97%)
Total Return: 45.97%

Year: 2012
2011 Net Asset Value: $37.20
Dividend Distribution: $.12 (0.32%)
2012 Net Asset Value: $45.69 (22.82%)
Total Return: 23.15%

Year: 2011
2010 Net Asset Value: $42.08
Dividend Distribution: $.00 (0.00%)
2011 Net Asset Value: $37.20 (-11.60)
Total Return: -11.60%

Year: 2010
2009 Net Asset Value: $29.40
Dividend Distribution: $.05 (0.17%)
2010 Net Asset Value: $42.08 (43.13%)
Total Return: 43.30%

Averages	Dividends	Performance	Total Return
Five years	5.03%	17.36%	22.40%
Three years	8.33%	18.42%	26.76%
Two years	12.34%	16.22%	28.56%

Telecommunication (TEL)
Price Media & Telecom – PRMTX
800-638-5660

T. Rowe Price Funds
100 E. Pratt St.
Baltimore, MD 21202

Net Asset Value: $68.77
Dividend Distribution: $0.00
Total Return 4/10/15: 5.69%
Risk: High
Minimum investment purchase: $2500
Minimum IRA purchase: $1000
Maximum front end sales load: None
Date of Inception: October 13, 1993
Number of Years of Gains: 15
Number of Years of Losses: 6
Net Expense Ratio: 0.80%
Category Average Net Expense Ratio: 1.54%

FIVE YEAR ANNUAL RETURNS:

Year: 2014
2013 Net Asset Value: $69.46
Dividend Distribution: $7.27   (10.46%)
2014 Net Asset Value: $65.07
Performance: -6.32%
Category Rank: 14%
Total Return: 4.14%

Year: 2013
2012 Net Asset Value: $53.30
Dividend Distribution: $5.58   (10.46%)
2013 Net Asset Value: $69.46   (30.32%)
Total Return: 40.78%

Year: 2012
2011 Net Asset Value: $46.91
Dividend Distribution: $4.25   (9.07%)
2012 Net Asset Value: $53.30   (13.62%)
Total Return: 22.69%

Year: 2011
2010 Net Asset Value: $51.12
Dividend Distribution: $4.65   (8.99%)
2011 Net Asset Value: $46.91   (-9.30%)
Total Return: -0.31%

Year: 2010
2009 Net Asset Value: $41.03
Dividend Distribution: $.30   (0.73%)
2010 Net Asset Value: $51.72   (26 .05%)
Total Return: 26.79%

Averages	Dividends	Performance	Total Return
Five years	7.94%	10.87%	18.82%
Three years	10.00%	12.54%	22.54%
Two years	10.46%	12.00%	22.46%

Utility (UT)
Hennessy Gas Utility Index - GASFX
888-888-0025

Hennessy Funds
7250 Redwood Blvd.
Novato CA 94945

Net Asset Value: $30.12
Dividend Distribution: $.18
Total Return 4/10/15: -0.68%
Risk: Average
Minimum Investment Purchase: $1000
Minimum IRA Purchase: N/A
Maximum Front End Sales Load: None
Date of Inception: May 10, 1989
Number of Years of Gains: 19
Number of Years of Losses: 6
Net Expense Ratio: 0.80%
Category Average Net Expense Ratio: 1.28%

FIVE YEAR ANNUAL RETURNS:

Year: 2014
2013 Net Asset Value: $26.50
Dividend Distribution: $1.61   (6.07%)
2014 Net Asset Value: $30.51
Performance: 15.13%
Category Rank: 34%
Total Return: 21.20%

Year: 2013
2012 Net Asset Value: $22.13
Dividend Distribution: $1.25   (5.67%)
2013 Net Asset Value: $26.50   (19.75%)
Total Return: 25.42%

Year: 2012
2011 Net Asset Value: $21.70
Dividend Distribution: $1.19   (5.47%)
2012 Net Asset Value: $22.13   (1.98%)
Total Return: 7.45%

Year: 2011
2010 Net Asset Value: $17.91
Dividend Distribution: $.71   (3.99%)
2011 Net Asset Value: $21.70   (21.16%)
Total Return: 25.15%

Year: 2010
2009 Net Asset Value: $16.76
Dividend Distribution: $.93   (5.54%)
2010 Net Asset Value: $17.91   (6.86%)
Total Return: 12.40%

Averages	Dividends	Performance	Total Return
Five years	5.35%	12.98%	18.33%
Three years	5.74%	12.29%	18.03%
Two years	5.87%	17.44%	23.31%

BOND FUND REPORTS

Here are eight successful bond mutual funds. The same mutual fund principles, the criteria of performance, distribution and risk was used.

The data is gathered from reliable sources and we are confident of the data researched. There is no guarantee of completeness and accuracy. Mutual fund performances and returns are based on the last market closing date in December.

There is no guarantee of future results. Always contact the mutual fund and read the prospectus before making any investment.

71

Corporate Grade A Debt (CA)
Eaton Vance National Muni A - EANAX
800-262-1122

Eaton Vance Municipals
Two International Place
Boston, MA 02110

Net Asset Value: $9.91
Dividend Distribution: $.10
Total Return: 0.89%
Risk: High
Minimum Investment Purchase: $1000
Minimum IRA Purchase: N/A
Maximum Front End Sales Load: 4.75%
Date of Inception: April 5, 1994
Number of Years of Gains: 15
Number of Years of Losses: 5
Net Expense Ratio: 0.71%
Category Average Net Expense Ratio: 0.90%

FIVE YEAR ANNUAL RETURNS

Year: 2014
2013 Net Asset Value: $9.04
Dividend Distribution: $.45   (4.97%)
2014 Net Asset Value: $9.93
Performance: 9.85%
Category Rank: 4%
Total Return: 14.81%

Year: 2013
2012 Net Asset Value: $10.26
Dividend Distribution: $.49 (4.73%)
2013 Net Asset Value: $9.04 (-11.89%)
Total Return: -7.16%

Year: 2012
2011 Net Asset Value: $9.41
Dividend Distribution: $.49 (5.17%)
2012 Net Asset Value: $10.26 (9.03%)
Total Return: 14.20%

Year: 2011
2010 Net Asset Value: $8.92
Dividend Distribution: $.55 (6.20%)
2011 Net Asset Value: $9.41 (5.49%)
Total Return: 11.69%

Year: 2010
2009 Net Asset Value: $9.53
Dividend Distribution: $.50 (5.26%)
2010 Net Asset Value: $8.92 (-6.40%)
Total Return: -1.14%

Averages	Dividends	Performance	Total Return
Five years	5.26%	1.22%	6.48%
Three years	4.96%	2.33%	7.29%
Two years	4.85%	-1.02%	3.83%

Corporate Invest BBB Debt (CB)
Delaware Ext. Duration Bond A– DEEAX
800-523-1918

Delaware Group Income Funds
One Commerce Square, 2005 Market Street
Philadelphia, PA 19103

Net Asset Value: $ 6 . 7 8
Dividend Distribution: $.06
Total Return 4/10/15: 3.48%
Risk: Average
Minimum Investment Purchase: $1000
Minimum IRA Purchase: $250
Maximum Front End Sales Load: 4.50%
Date of Inception: September 15, 1988
Number of Years of Gains: 13
Number of Years of Losses: 3
Net Expense Ratio: 0.96%
Category Average Net Expense Ratio: 0.85%

FIVE YEAR ANNUAL RETURNS

Year: 2014
2013 Net Asset Value: $6.23
Dividend Distribution: $.60   (9.61%)
2014 Net Asset Value: $6.62
Performance: 6.26%
Category Rank: 6%
Total Return: 15.87%

Year: 2013
2012 Net Asset Value: $6.79
Dividend Distribution: $.29   (4.20%)
2013 Net Asset Value: $6.23   (-8.25%)
Total Return: -4.05%

Year: 2012
2011 Net Asset Value: $6.49
Dividend Distribution: $.76   (11.76%)
2012 Net Asset Value: $6.79   (4.62%)
Total Return: 16.38%

Year: 2011
2010 Net Asset Value: $6.11
Dividend Distribution: $.62   (10.21%)
2011 Net Asset Value: $6.49   (6.22%)
Total Return: 16.43%

Year: 2010
2009 Net Asset Value: $5.94
Dividend Distribution: $.68   (11.39%)
2010 Net Asset Value: $6.11   (2.86%)
Total Return: 14.25%

Averages	Dividends	Performance	Total Return
Five years	9.44%	2.34%	11.78%
Three years	8.53%	0.88%	9.41%
Two years	6.92%	-0.99%	5.91%

General Municipal (GM)
Western Asset Managed Muni A– SHMMX
877-721-1926

Legg Mason & Company, LLC
55 Water Street, 32nd Floor
New York, NY 10004

Net Asset Value: $ 1 6 . 9 2
Dividend Distribution: $.18
Total Return: 1.31%
Risk: Average
Minimum Investment Purchase: $1000
Minimum IRA Purchase: N/A
Maximum Front End Sales Load: 4.25%
Date of Inception: March 4, 1981
Number of Years of Gains: 29
Number of Years of Losses: 4
Net Expense Ratio: 0.66%
Category Average Net Expense Ratio: 0.90%

FIVE YEAR ANNUAL RETURNS

Year: 2014
2013 Net Asset Value: $15.83
Dividend Distribution: $.68   (4.28%)
2014 Net Asset Value: $16.88
Performance: 6.63%
Category Rank: 38%
Total Return: 10.91%

Year: 2013
2012 Net Asset Value: $17.23
Dividend Distribution: $.65   (3.77%)
2013 Net Asset Value: $15.83   (-8.13%)
Total Return: -4.36%

Year: 2012
2011 Net Asset Value: $16.27
Dividend Distribution: $.71   (4.35%)
2012 Net Asset Value: $17.23   (5.90%)
Total Return: 10.25%

Year: 2011
2010 Net Asset Value: $15.10
Dividend Distribution: $.77   (5.12%)
2011 Net Asset Value: $16.27   (7.75%)
Total Return: 12.87%

Year: 2010
2009 Net Asset Value: $15.81
Dividend Distribution: $.72   (4.56%)
2010 Net Asset Value: $15.10   (-4.49%)
Total Return: 0.07%

Averages	Dividends	Performance	Total Return
Five years	4.41%	1.53%	5.95%
Three years	4.13%	1.47%	5.60%
Two years	4.02%	-0.75%	3.28%

General U.S. Government (GG)
Morgan Stanley U.S. Govt A USGAX
800-869-6397

Morgan Stanley Funds
522 5th Ave.
New York, NY 10036

Net Asset Value: $8.92
Dividend Distribution: $.05
Total Return 4/10/15: 0.80%
Risk: Above Average
Minimum Investment Purchase: $1000
Minimum IRA Purchase: N/A
Maximum Front End Sales Load: 4.25%
Date of Inception: July 28, 1997
Number of Years of Gains: 14
Number of Years of Losses: 3
Net Expense Ratio: 0.89%
Category Average Net Expense Ratio: 0.92%

FIVE YEAR ANNUAL RETURNS

Year: 2014
2013 Net Asset Value: $8.63
Dividend Distribution: $.21   (2.47%)
2014 Net Asset Value: $8.90
Performance: 3.13%
Category Rank: 13%
Total Return: 5.60%

Year: 2013
2012 Net Asset Value: $9.03
Dividend Distribution: $.21   (2.33%)
2013 Net Asset Value: $8.63   (-4.43%)
Total Return: -2.10%

Year: 2012
2011 Net Asset Value: $8.91
Dividend Distribution: $.22   (2.51%)
2012 Net Asset Value: $9.03   (1.35%)
Total Return: 3.86%

Year: 2011
2010 Net Asset Value: $8.57
Dividend Distribution: $.31   (3.57%)
2011 Net Asset Value: $8.91   (3.97%)
Total Return: 7.54%

Year: 2010
2009 Net Asset Value: $8.41
Dividend Distribution: $.26   (3.13%)
2010 Net Asset Value: $8.57   (1.90%)
Total Return: 5.03%

Averages	Dividends	Performance	Total Return
Five years	2.80%	1.18%	3.98%
Three years	2.44%	0.01%	2.45%
Two years	2.40%	-0.65%	1.75%

High Yield Municipal (HY)
Invesco Hi-Yield Muni A - ACTHX
800-959-4246

AIM Investment Funds
11 Greenway Plaza – Suite 100
Houston, TX 77046

Net Asset Value: $10.08
Dividend Distribution: $.12
Total Return: 2.29%
Risk: Above Average
Minimum Investment Purchase: $1000
Minimum IRA Purchase: $250
Maximum Front End Sales Load: 4.25%
Date of Inception: January 2, 1986
Number of Years of Gains: 23
Number of Years of Losses: 5
Net Expense Ratio: 0.87%
Category Average Net Expense Ratio: 0.99%

FIVE YEAR ANNUAL RETURNS

Year: 2014
2013 Net Asset Value: $9.04
Dividend Distribution: $1.00   (11.04%)
2014 Net Asset Value: $9.99
Performance: 10.51%
Category Rank: 20%
Total Return: 21.55%

Year: 2013
2012 Net Asset Value: $10.12
Dividend Distribution: $.52   (5.11%)
2013 Net Asset Value: $9.04   (-10.67%)
Total Return: -5.56%

Year: 2012
2011 Net Asset Value: $9.40
Dividend Distribution: $.59   (6.26%)
2012 Net Asset Value: $10.12   (7.66%)
Total Return: 13.92%

Year: 2011
2010 Net Asset Value: $8.98
Dividend Distribution: $.59   (6.58%)
2011 Net Asset Value: $9.40   (4.68%)
Total Return: 11.26%

Year: 2010
2009 Net Asset Value: $9.13
Dividend Distribution: $.55   (5.99%)
2010 Net Asset Value: $8.98   ($-1.64)
Total Return: 4.35%

Averages	Dividends	Performance	Total Return
Five years	7.00%	2.11%	9.10%
Three years	7.47%	2.50%	9.97%
Two years	8.07%	-0.08%	7.99%

Intermediate Invest Grade Debt (IG)
Virtus Bond A - SAVAX
800-243-1574

Virtus Funds
100 Pearl St.
Hartford, CT 06103

Net Asset Value: $11.48
Dividend Distribution: $.11
Total Return: 2.21%
Risk: Average
Minimum Investment Purchase: $2500
Minimum IRA Purchase: $100
Maximum Front End Sales Load: 3.75%
Date of Inception: July 1, 1998
Number of Years of Gains: 15
Number of Years of Losses: 1
Net Expense Ratio: 0.85%
Category Average Net Expense Ratio: 0.87%

FIVE YEAR ANNUAL RETURNS

Year: 2014
2013 Net Asset Value: $11.30
Dividend Distribution: $.45   (4.02%)
2014 Net Asset Value: $11.24
Performance: -0.53%
Category Rank: 89%
Total Return: 3.49%

Year: 2013
2012 Net Asset Value: $11.68
Dividend Distribution: $.45   (3.87%)
2013 Net Asset Value: $11.30   (-3.25%)
Total Return: 0.62%

Year: 2012
2011 Net Asset Value: $11.13
Dividend Distribution: $.36   (3.23%)
2012 Net Asset Value: $11.68   (4.94%)
Total Return: 8.17%

Year: 2011
2010 Net Asset Value: $11.00
Dividend Distribution: $.48   (4.34%)
2011 Net Asset Value: $11.13   (1.18%)
Total Return: 5.52%

Year: 2010
2009 Net Asset Value: $10.58
Dividend Distribution: $.49   (4.61%)
2010 Net Asset Value: $11.00   (3.97%)
Total Return: 8.58%

Averages	Dividends	Performance	Total Return
Five years	4.01%	1.26%	5.27%
Three years	3.71%	0.39%	4.10%
Two years	3.95%	-1.89%	2.04%

US Government Mortgage (MT)
Columbia U.S. Govt Mortage A- AUGAX
800.345.6611

Columbia Mgt Investment Services, Corp.
P.O. Box 8081
Boston, MA 02266-8081

Net Asset Value: $5.56
Dividend Distribution: $.04
Total Return: 1.44%
Risk: Average
Minimum Investment Purchase: $2000
Minimum IRA Purchase: $1000
Maximum Front End Sales Load: 4.75%
Date of Inception: February 14, 2002
Number of Years of Gains: 10
Number of Years of Losses: 2
Net Expense Ratio: 0.86%
Category Average Net Expense Ratio: 0.92%

FIVE YEAR ANNUAL RETURNS

Year: 2014
2013 Net Asset Value: $5.37
Dividend Distribution: $.15   (2.72%)
2014 Net Asset Value: $5.52
Performance: 2.79%
Category Rank: 49%
Total Return: 5.51%

85

Year: 2013
2012 Net Asset Value: $5.62
Dividend Distribution: $.16   (2.91%)
2013 Net Asset Value: $5.37   (-4.45%)
Total Return: -1.54%

Year: 2012
2011 Net Asset Value: $5.52
Dividend Distribution: $.28   (5.14%)
2012 Net Asset Value: $5.62   (1.81%)
Total Return: 6.95%

Year: 2011
2010 Net Asset Value: $5.25
Dividend Distribution: $.19   (3.64%)
2011 Net Asset Value: $5.52   (5.14%)
Total Return: 8.78%

Year: 2010
2009 Net Asset Value: $4.98
Dividend Distribution: $.24   (4.85%)
2010 Net Asset Value: $5.25   (5.42%)
Total Return: 10.27%

Averages	Dividends	Performance	Total Return
Five years	3.85%	2.14%	5.99%
Three years	3.59%	0.05%	3.64%
Two years	2.82%	-0.83%	1.99%

Multi-Sector (MS)
PIMCO Income Fund A - PONAX
800-243-1574

PIMCO Income Fund
840 Newport Center Dr.
Newport Beach CA 92660

Net Asset Value: $12.50
Dividend Distribution: $.16
Total Return 4/10/15: 2.80%
Risk: Below Average
Minimum Investment Purchase: $1000
Minimum IRA Purchase: $1000
Maximum Front End Sales Load: 3.75%
Date of Inception: March 30, 2007
Number of Years of Gains: 6
Number of Years of Losses: 1
Net Expense Ratio: 0.85%
Category Average Net Expense Ratio: 1.07%

FIVE YEAR ANNUAL RETURNS

Year: 2014
2013 Net Asset Value: $12.26
Dividend Distribution: $.76   (6.21%)
2014 Net Asset Value: $12.33
Performance: 0.57%
Category Rank: 6%
Total Return: 6.78%

Year: 2013
2012 Net Asset Value: $12.36
Dividend Distribution: $.65   (5.23%)
2013 Net Asset Value: $12.26   (-0.81%)
Total Return: 4.42%

Year: 2012
2011 Net Asset Value: $10.85
Dividend Distribution: $.85   (7.79%)
2012 Net Asset Value: $12.36   (13.92%)
Total Return: 21.71%

Year: 2011
2010 Net Asset Value: $11.04
Dividend Distribution: $.84   (7.64%)
2011 Net Asset Value: $10.85   (-1.72%)
Total Return: 5.92%

Year: 2010
2009 Net Asset Value: $9.84
Dividend Distribution: $.71   (7.18%)
2010 Net Asset Value: $11.04   (12.20%)
Total Return: 9.38%

Averages	Dividends	Performance	Total Return
Five years	6.81%	4.83%	11.64%
Three years	6.41%	4.56%	10.97%
Two years	5.72%	-0.12%	5.60%

RETIREMENT PROSPERITY

 The following verifiable hypothesis illustrates the growth of investment performance and reinvestment_of an active Multi-Sector Bond fund, Columbia Strategic Income Fund: A – COSIX, which is open to all investors.

The model shows:
1) Initial nest egg investment
2) Purchased net asset value share price
3) Fees incurred
4) Number of shares purchased
5) Number of shares reinvested
6) Performances
7) Total returns
8) Reinvested share price

This Bond fund portfolio shows the actual distribution investors received and benefits incurred when the income is reinvested every month.

The model represents a $2,000 initial investment made on January 1, 2012. Another $2000 investment being made January 1, 2013. Finally, the investor turns 70 1/2 years of age on January 1, 2014.

Investment & Reinvestment MODEL

January 2, 2012 INITIAL PURCHASE

Investment Category: Multi-Sector Bond
Minimum Purchase (Nest Egg): $2,000
Net Asset Value (Purchase Price): $6.05
Maximum Sales Fees (Fees): 4.75%
Date of Inception: April 21, 1977
Risk: Below Average
Number of Years of Gains: 33
Number of Years of Losses: 4
Net Expense Ratio: 1.03%
Category Average Net Expense Ratio: 1.07%

Total Shares purchased: 314.876
Investment Value: $1,905.00 -$95.00 (-4.75%)

December 31, 2012 End of Year Overview:

Net Asset Value : $6.42
Total Performance: 6.12%
Total Distribution of Income: $85.20   (4.26%)
Total Shares Owned: 329.0540
Total Return on Investment: $2,112.53   (5.63%)

<<Continues>>

90

****

January 2, 2013 ADDITIONAL PURCHASE

Investment (Nest Egg): $2,000.00
Net Asset Value (Purchased): $6.43
Fees: -4.75%   ($95.00)
Additional Shares Purchased: 296.2674
Total Combined Shares: 625.3214

December 31, 2013 End of Year End Overview:

Net Asset Value: $6.00
Total Performance: -6.54%
Total Distribution of Income: $271.49   (6.78%)
Total Shares Owned: 669.5938
Total Return on Investment: $4,017.56   0.43%

<<Continues>>

The model continues into 2014; however, this hypothesis is based on an investor's return who is 70½ years of age on January 2, 2014 and cannot purchase any more shares for his/her IRA portfolio.

91

■■■■■■■■■■■■■■■■■■■■■■■<<<■■■■■■■■■■■■■■■■■■■■■■■■■■■■

2014 Distribution & Re-Investment Only

Total Shares Owned 1/1/2014: 669.5938

1/24/2014 Income Distribution: $.018 per share
Net Asset Value: $6.01
Total Distribution Value: $12.0526
Shares Reinvested: 2.0054
Total Shares Owned: 671.5992

2/25/2014 Income Distribution: $.018 per share
Net Asset Value: $6.07
Total Distribution Value: $12.0887
Shares Reinvested: 1.9915
Total Shares Owned: 673.5907

3/24/2014 Income Distribution: $.018 per share
Net Asset Value: $6.09
Total Distribution Value: $11.3190
Shares Reinvested: 1.9909
Total Shares Owned: 675.5816

4/25/2014 Income Distribution: $.018 per share
Net Asset Value: $6.14
Total Distribution Value: $12.6104
Shares Reinvested: 1.9805
Total Shares Owned: 677.5621

<<Continues>>

5/23/2014 Income Distribution: $.018 per share
Net Asset Value: $6.17
Total Distribution Value: $12.1961
Shares Reinvested: 1.9766
Total Shares Owned: 679.5387

6/25/2014 Income Distribution: $.018 per share
Net Asset Value: $6.21
Total Distribution Value: $12.2316
Shares Reinvested: 1.9696
Total Shares Owned: 681.5083

7/25/2014 Income Distribution: $.018 per share
Net Asset Value: $6.21
Total Distribution Value: $12.2671
Shares Reinvested: 1.9753
Total Shares Owned: 683.4836

8/25/2014 Income Distribution: $.018 per share
Net Asset Value: $6.20
Total Distribution Value: $12.3027
Shares Reinvested: 1.9843
Total Shares Owned: 685.4679

9/24/2014 Income Distribution: $0.018 per share Net
Asset Value: $6.13
Total Value of Distribution: $12.3384
Shares reinvested: 2.0127
Total Shares Owned: 687.4806

<<Continues>>

10/24/2014 Income Distribution: $0.018 per share
Net Asset Value: $6.10
Total Distribution Value: $12.3746
Shares Reinvested: 2.0286
Total uses Shares Owned: 689.5092

11/25/2014 Income Distribution: $0.018 per share
Net Asset Value: $6.08
Total Distribution Value: $12.4111
Shares Reinvested: 2.0412
Total Shares Owned: 691.5504

12/17/2014 Income Distribution: $.141 per share
Net Asset Value: $5.79
Total Distribution Value: $97.5086
Shares Reinvested: 16.8408
Total Shares Owned: 708.3912

December 31, 2014   End of Year Overview:
Total Portfolio Investment: $4,000.00
Net Asset Value: $5.88
Total Distribution of Income: $231 .70   (5.79%)
Total Shares Reinvested: 38.7974
Total Shares Owned: 708.3912
Total Return: $ 4 1 6 5 . 3 4 (4 . 1 3 %)

* * * * * * * * * * * * *

About the Author:

King Kovacs, is also the CEO/Founder of Mutual Interest Data Service, Ltd.

Being the Executive Administrator, he maintains two Websites; www.largedividends.com and www.retirement-investments101.com.

An expert author on Ezine Articles.com,King has published several investment articles on Mutual Funds. Graduating from Rider University with a degree in Business Administration, he resides in New Jersey with his wife, Claire and family.

KingKovacs1 - Twitter
(www.twitter.com/**kingkovacs1**)

Made in the USA
Middletown, DE
25 May 2015